EXPLORING
THE
PLANETS
in Our Solar System

The Rosen Publishing Group's
PowerKids Press™
New York

REBECCA OLIEN

Published in 2007 by The Rosen Publishing Group, Inc.
29 East 21st Street, New York, NY 10010

First Edition

Editor: Amelie von Zumbusch
Book Design: Ginny Chu

Photo Credits: Cover, pp. 4, 6, 12 © Detlev Van Ravenswaay/Photo Researchers, Inc.; p. 8, Courtesy NASA/JPL-Caltech; p. 10 NASA Earth Observatory; p.14 NASA/JPL/Space Science Institute; p. 16 © Chris Butler/Photo Researchers, Inc.; p. 18 © Mark Garlick/Photo Researchers, Inc.; p. 20 NASA

Library of Congress Cataloging-in-Publication Data

Olien, Rebecca.
  Exploring the planets in our solar system / Rebecca Olien.— 1st ed.
      p. cm. — (Objects in the sky)
  Includes index.
  ISBN 1-4042-3467-5 (library binding) — ISBN 1-4042-2175-1 (pbk.) — ISBN 1-4042-2366-5 (six pack)
  1. Solar system—Juvenile literature. 2. Planets—Juvenile literature. I. Title. II. Series.

QB501.3.O45 2007
523.4—dc22
                                                                                    2005035106

Manufactured in the United States of America

CONTENTS

This drawing shows the eight planets in our solar system. The wide band between Mars and Jupiter is a group of rocks that orbits the Sun.

The Solar System

A solar system is made of a star and the objects that circle it. The largest of these objects are planets. The Sun is the star at the center of our solar system. Eight planets circle the Sun in paths called **orbits**.

The planets closest to the Sun are called inner planets. Mercury, Venus, Earth, and Mars are inner planets. Jupiter, Saturn, Uranus, and Neptune are outer planets. They are not as close to the Sun. The inner planets are made of rock. The outer planets are made mostly of gas.

There is no water on Mercury, but there is ice inside some of the planet's craters.

Mercury

Mercury is the planet closest to the Sun. The Sun's heat can make Mercury very hot. Parts of Mercury's **surface** facing the Sun reach more than 800° F (430° C). However, the side of Mercury that faces away from the Sun gets very cold. The **temperature** there can fall to about -300° F (-184° C).

Mercury is covered with **craters**. These craters were made by **meteorites** and **asteroids** that crashed into Mercury. The biggest craters are called basins. Caloris Basin is the largest basin on Mercury. It is more than 800 miles (1,287 km) wide.

Venus's atmosphere traps sunlight and makes the planet very hot. Its temperature reaches about 900° F (482° C).

VENUS

The planet Venus is one of the brightest objects in the night sky. Venus is so bright because it is covered by a thick **atmosphere** made mostly of **carbon dioxide** gas. This atmosphere reflects, or shines back, most sunlight that reaches it. The light that gets through Venus's atmosphere is trapped inside it. This makes Venus the hottest planet in the solar system.

Venus is the second planet from the Sun. Most of Venus's surface is covered in rock made by volcanoes. Volcanoes are mountains that shoot out melted rock.

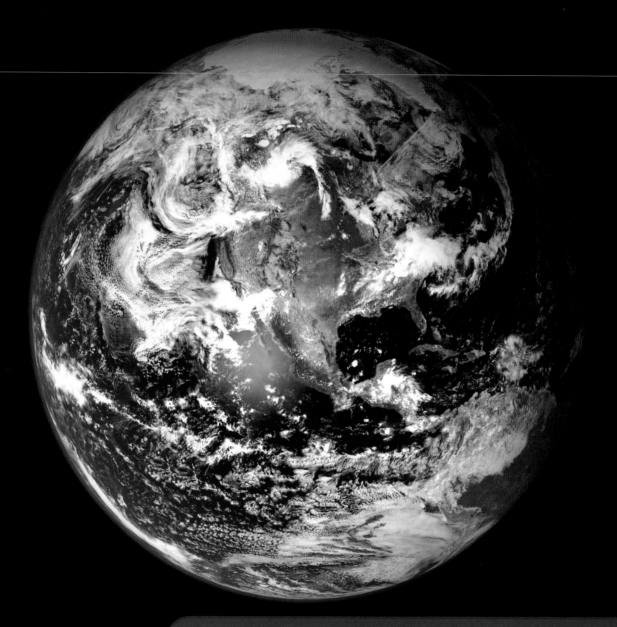

Water is very important for life on Earth. The first living things were formed in the oceans.

EARTH

Earth is our solar system's third planet. It orbits 91 million miles (146 million km) from the Sun. Earth's orbit takes about 365 days, or one year. As it orbits the Sun, Earth spins around once every 24 hours. This spinning causes day and night.

Earth has everything needed for life. Earth's atmosphere holds oxygen, a gas animals need to breathe. Its atmosphere also keeps Earth from getting too hot or too cold. Over half of Earth's surface is covered by water. This is important because all animals and plants need water to live.

Olympus Mons, shown above, is 17 miles (27 km) tall. It is three times taller than Mount Everest, the highest mountain on Earth.

Mars

Mars is known as the red planet because of its many red rocks. These rocks are red because they have iron oxide, or rust, in them. The planet Mars is named after Mars the Roman god of war because of the planet's red color. This is because red is the color of blood, and war is bloody.

Mars is the fourth planet from the Sun. It has many craters and volcanoes. Olympus Mons is a volcano on Mars. It is the tallest known mountain in the solar system. Most of Mars is dry and rocky, but it has ice at its two **poles**.

The Great
Red Spot

The Great Red Spot is the largest
storm in our solar system. It is at
least two times wider than Earth.

Jupiter

Jupiter is larger than all the other planets put together. It measures about 88,846 miles (142,984 km) in **diameter**. Jupiter is the fifth planet from the Sun and the first of the outer planets.

Jupiter is made mostly of **hydrogen** and **helium** gas. Yellow, red, and brown stripes, called belts and zones, ring the planet. The belts and zones are made from clouds of gas and ice.

Jupiter is a stormy planet. One large storm is called the Great Red Spot. This storm has lasted for at least 300 years.

Saturn's rings are made of pieces of rock, dust, and ice. This picture shows how the rings look up close.

SATURN

The sixth planet from the Sun is Saturn. Saturn is almost two times as far from the Sun as Jupiter is. It is about 887 million miles (1.4 billion km) from the Sun. Like other outer planets, Saturn is made mostly of hydrogen and helium. It is the second-largest planet in the solar system.

Saturn is known for its bright, colorful rings. The rings look bright because they reflect a lot of light. Along with the rings, 47 moons orbit Saturn. Saturn's biggest moon, Titan, is larger than the planet Mercury.

Uranus has 13 rings. The rings circle around Uranus from top to bottom rather than from side to side. This is because Uranus spins on its side.

Uranus

Uranus is the only planet to spin on its side. It takes Uranus 84 years to orbit the Sun. During this time the poles of Uranus change places once. This gives the poles 42 years of light followed by 42 years of darkness. **Scientists** believe Uranus may have crashed with a large object long ago. This crash caused Uranus to spin in this way.

Uranus is the seventh planet from the Sun. It gets little of the Sun's warmth and is very cold. The temperature on Uranus is near -357° F (-216° C).

Neptune is the farthest planet from the Sun. This is why it is so cold.

Neptune

Neptune is covered by clouds of **methane** gas. The methane gives Neptune a blue color. Neptune is a windy planet. Winds on Neptune blow more than 1,200 miles per hour (1,931 km/h). Neptune is also very cold. The temperature there can fall to around -360° F (-218° C).

Neptune has about a dozen moons. The largest of these moons is Triton. Triton is even colder than Neptune is. It can get as cold as -400° F (-240° C) on Triton. It is so cold that there are ice volcanoes there.

Pluto and Other Dwarf Planets

A band of icy rocks called the Kuiper Belt lies past Neptune. Pluto is one of the objects in the Kuiper Belt. People used to consider Pluto a planet. However, in August 2006, scientists named Pluto a dwarf planet.

Dwarf planets are smaller than true planets. Dwarf planets share their orbits with other objects. For example, the dwarf planet Ceres shares its orbit with the **asteroid belt**.

Scientists think we have not yet discovered all the dwarf planets. We still have much to learn about our solar system!

Glossary

asteroids (AS-teh-roydz) Small bodies made of rock and iron that travel around the Sun.

asteroid belt (AS-teh-royd BELT) A band of rocks that travel around the Sun between Mars and Jupiter.

atmosphere (AT-muh-sfeer) The gas around an object in space.

carbon dioxide (KAR-bin dy-OK-syd) A gas that plants take in from the air and use to make food.

craters (KRAY-turz) Large holes on a moon or planet.

diameter (dy-A-meh-ter) The measurement across the center of a round object.

helium (HEE-lee-um) A light colorless gas.

hydrogen (HY-dreh-jen) A colorless gas that catches fire easily and weighs less than any other known kind of matter.

meteorites (MEE-tee-uh-ryts) Rocks from outer space that reach a planet's surface.

methane (MEH-thayn) A colorless gas.

orbits (OR-bits) The paths objects use to travel around a larger object.

poles (POHLZ) The two points least close to the center of a planet.

scientists (SY-un-tists) People who study the world.

temperature (TEM-pur-cher) How hot or cold something is.

Index

E
Earth, 5, 11

H
helium, 15, 17
hydrogen, 15, 17

J
Jupiter, 5, 15, 17

M
Mars, 5, 13
Mercury, 5, 7, 17
meteorites, 7

N
Neptune, 5, 21

P
Pluto, 22

S
Saturn, 5, 17
Sun, 5, 7, 9, 15, 19

U
Uranus, 5, 19

V
Venus, 5, 9

Web Sites

Due to the changing nature of Internet links, PowerKids Press has developed an online list of Web sites related to the subject of this book. This site is updated regularly. Please use this link to access the list: www.powerkidslinks.com/oits/planets/